Black Sabbath
Through The Seventies

Black Sabbath
Through The Seventies

WYMER
PUBLISHING
Bedford, England

First published in Great Britain in 2018
by Wymer Publishing
www.wymerpublishing.co.uk
Tel: 01234 326691
Wymer Publishing is a trading name of Wymer (UK) Ltd

Copyright © 2018 Wymer Publishing.

ISBN: 978-1-912782-03-1 (Hardback)
ISBN: 978-1-912782-06-2 (Paperback)

The Author hereby asserts his rights to be identified
as the author of this work in accordance with sections
77 to 78 of the Copyright, Designs & Patents Act 1988.

All rights reserved. No part of this publication may be
reproduced or transmitted in any form or by any means,
electronic or mechanical, including photocopying, or any
information storage and retrieval system, without written
permission from the publisher.

This publication is sold subject to the condition that it shall not,
by way of trade or otherwise, be lent, re-sold, hired out or
otherwise circulated without the publishers prior consent in any
form of binding or cover other than that in which it is published
and without a similar condition including this condition
being imposed on the subsequent purchaser.

Every effort has been made to trace the copyright holders of the
photographs in this book but some were unreachable. We would
be grateful if the photographers concerned would contact us.

Book Design by 1016 Sarpsborg
Typeset by The Andys.
Printed and bound in England by Harrier LLC.

A catalogue record for this book is available from the British Library.

Cover design by 1016 Sarpsborg
Front cover photo © Alan Perry

Back cover photo © Richard Galbraith.

The phrase "breaking the mould" is often used in many contexts but the phrase "creating the mould" is far less frequently used. But if one band can be put forward for creating a musical genre then it would be very hard to argue against Black Sabbath.

The Sabs, as they have lovingly become known, really were musical pioneers. I remember hearing the band's title track on that debut album when it was released in 1970 and I am hard pushed to think of any other piece of music that had such a huge impact. I tip my hat to rock journalist Malcolm Dome when he said, "'Black Sabbath' by Black Sabbath, starts, stops and defines heavy rock. Everything else is mere interpretation." I endorse those words fully. Who would disagree? I doubt any of you who have bought this book will.

As befitting one of the giants of rock, several books have been produced on the band, most seemingly focussing on the trials and tribulations and all the usual shenanigans that go hand in hand with rock bands... particularly rock bands during those heady days of the seventies when Sabbath and their contemporaries were in their element. Huge selling albums and countless tours went hand in hand with the lifestyle that followed. Sabbath were no exception and it really did take its toll, although thankfully they all still managed to come out of it at the other end.

But to fill another book with the same old stories was never our intention. Instead we just wanted to present a snapshot of the classic Sabbath days, the original line-up doing what it did best. Many of the photos within have never been published in a book before and make a wonderful souvenir of Sabbath in the seventies.

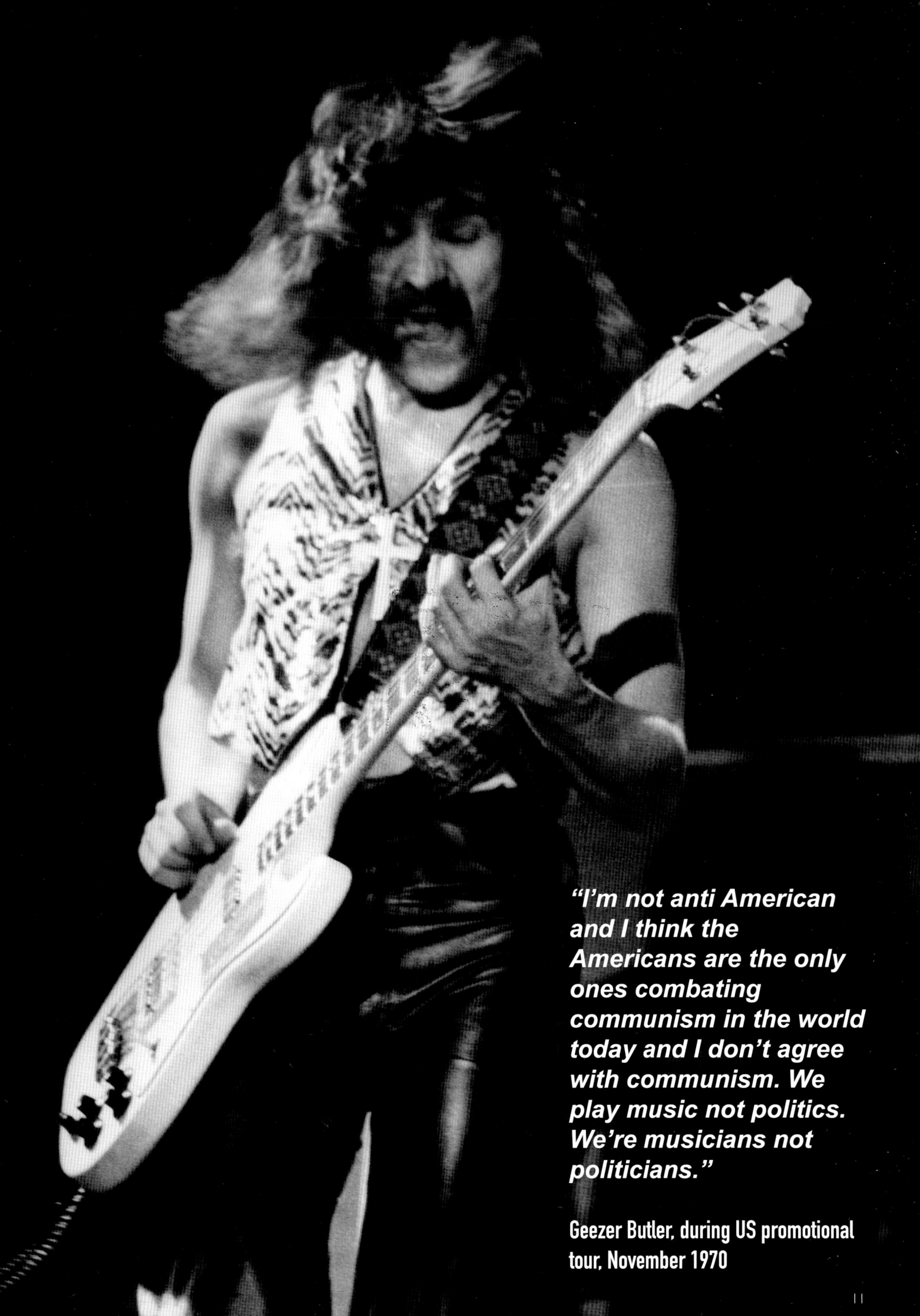

"I'm not anti American and I think the Americans are the only ones combating communism in the world today and I don't agree with communism. We play music not politics. We're musicians not politicians."

Geezer Butler, during US promotional tour, November 1970

"I'm very confused because in the last four or five years, my living standards are rising and rising, my whole way of life has changed. My whole outlook on people has changed too, not because I wanted it to, but because people have made it. You're isolated. People think you are rolling in money, they don't understand about the tax man and all that."

Ozzy Osbourne,
Sounds, 17th November 1973

"What does it in the States is that it's all the same, it's got no character. In America you can go to one city, travel a thousand miles to another place and it'll look more or less the same. The same sort of hotel — Holiday Inns and things like that, they're all basically the same — you can look out of the window and think 'where am I today?' You can lose touch of where you are today, where you were yesterday."

Bill Ward, Sounds, 6th January 1973

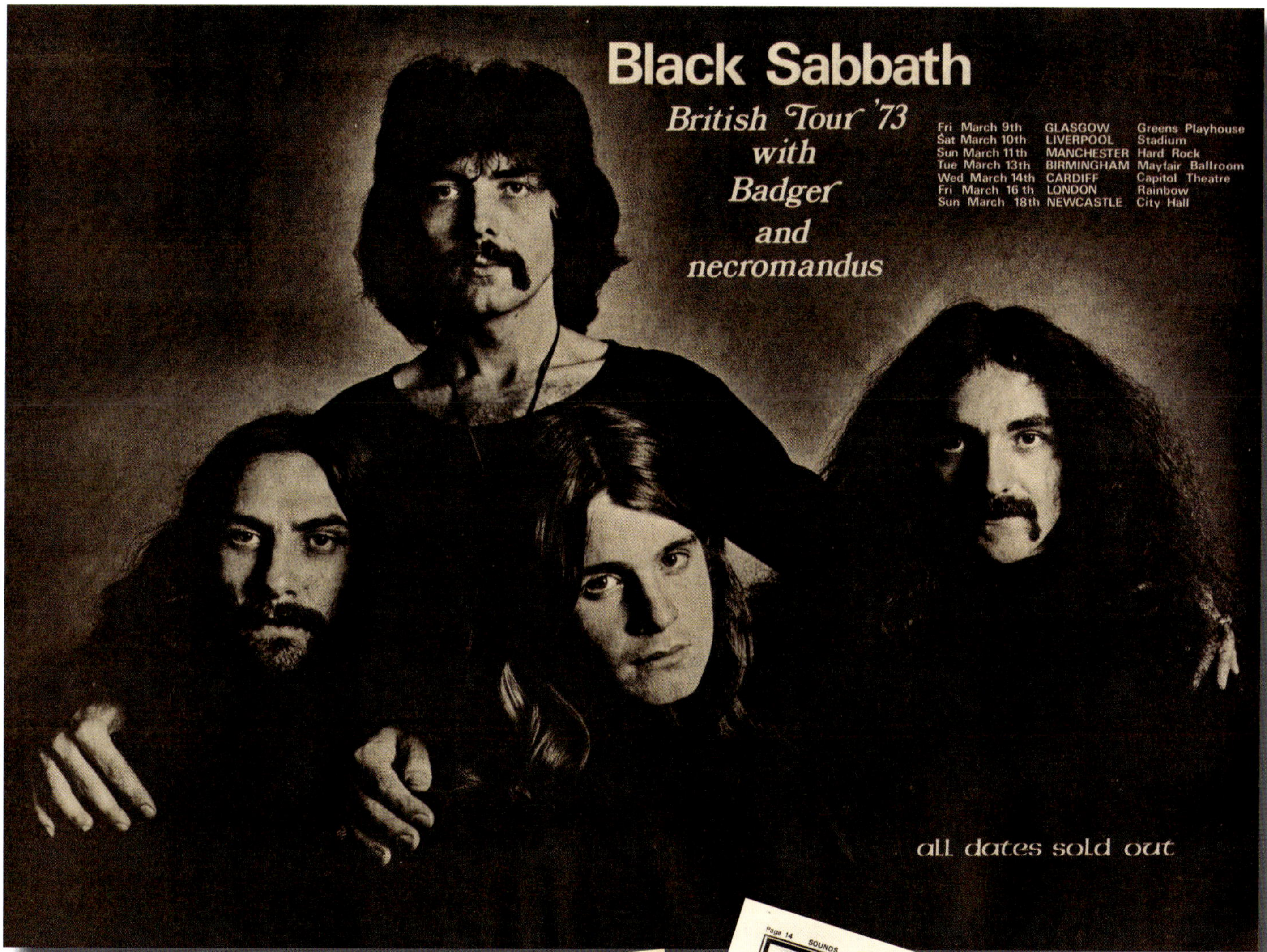

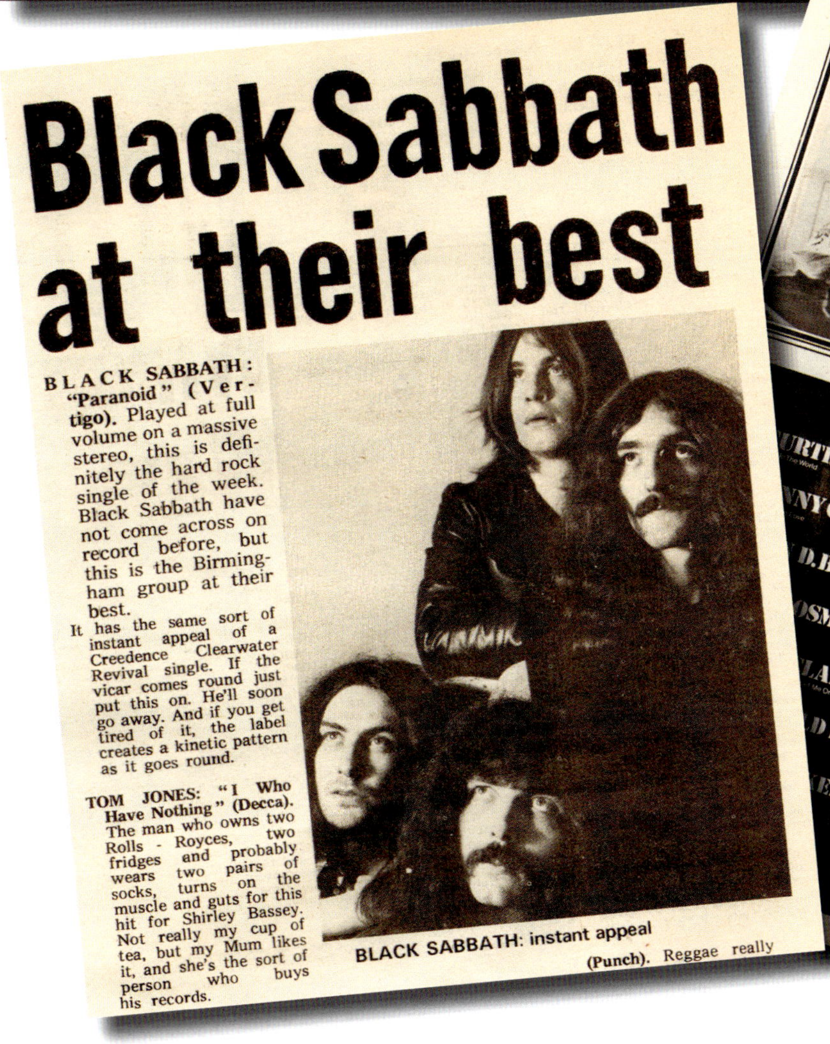

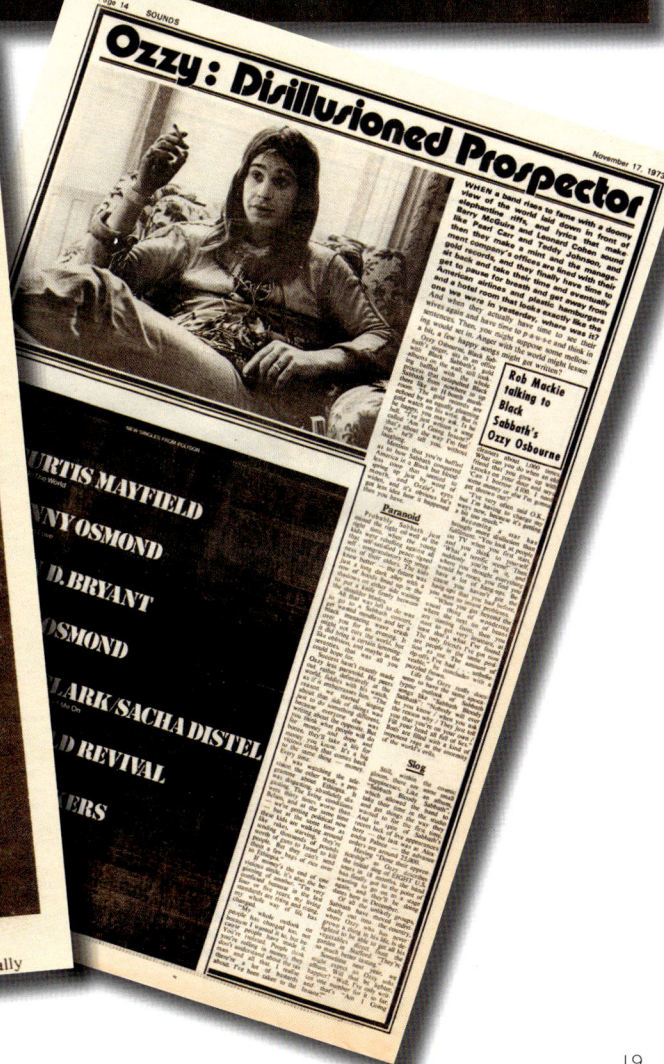

Black Sabbath at their best

BLACK SABBATH: "Paranoid" (Vertigo). Played at full volume on a massive stereo, this is definitely the hard rock single of the week. Black Sabbath have not come across on record before, but this is the Birmingham group at their best.

It has the same sort of instant appeal of a Creedence Clearwater Revival single. If the vicar comes round just put this on. He'll soon go away. And if you get tired of it, the label creates a kinetic pattern as it goes round.

TOM JONES: "I Who Have Nothing" (Decca). The man who owns two Rolls - Royces, two fridges and probably wears two pairs of socks, turns on the muscle and guts for this hit for Shirley Bassey. Not really my cup of tea, but my Mum likes it, and she's the sort of person who buys his records.

BLACK SABBATH: instant appeal

(Punch). Reggae really

Page 14 SOUNDS

November 17, 1973

Ozzy: Disillusioned Prospector

WHEN a band rises to fame with a doomy view of the world laid down in front of elephantine riffs, and lyrics that make Barry McGuire and Leonard Cohen sound like Pearl Carr and Teddy Johnson, and then they make a mint and the management company's offices are lined with their gold records, and they finally have time to sit back and take their time and eventually get to pause for breath and get away from American airlines and plastic hamburgers and a hotel room that looks exactly like the one we were in yesterday, where was it? And when they actually have time to see their wives again and have time to p-a-u-s-e and think in sentences. Then, you might suppose some mellowing would set in. Anger with the world might lessen a bit, a few happy songs might get written?

Rob Mackie talking to Black Sabbath's Ozzy Osbourne

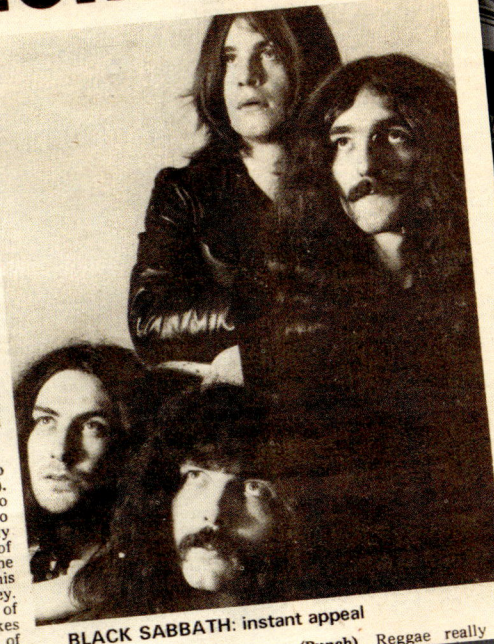

"I think a lot of people are under the impression that being a superstar is just great, but it's not you know, it's nice to live a different life sometimes. When we finish a tour we all go home and live different lives because the hassle of being known can be really bad sometimes. People find out your phone number or where you live and although it's nice to talk to the people, they don't understand you've just being doing a tour and all you want to do is relax."

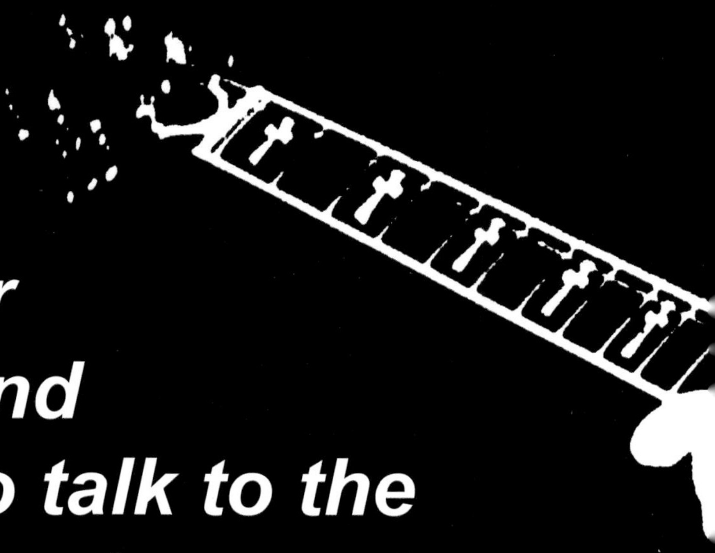

Tony Iommi, Sounds, 6th January 1973

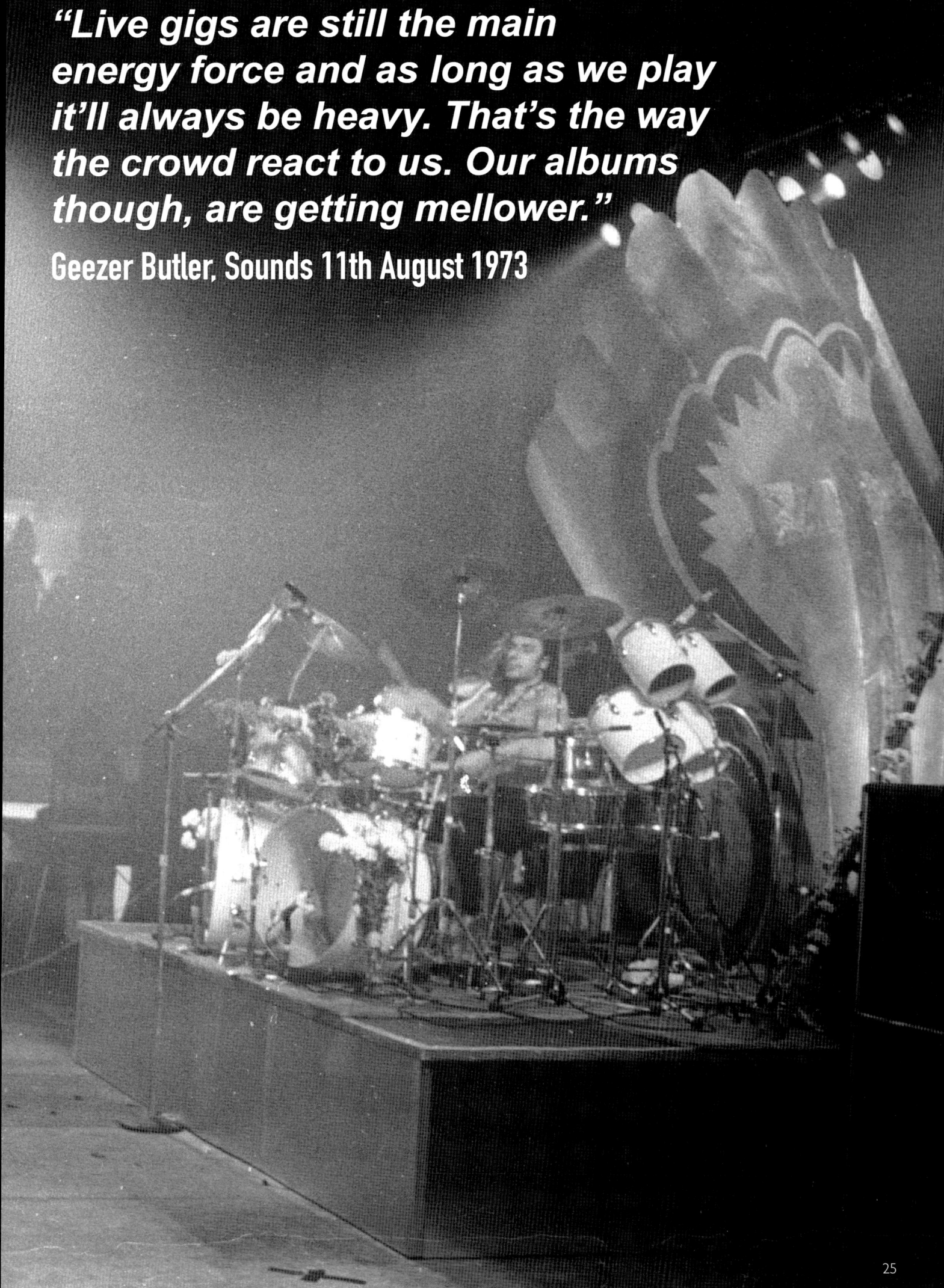

"Live gigs are still the main energy force and as long as we play it'll always be heavy. That's the way the crowd react to us. Our albums though, are getting mellower."

Geezer Butler, Sounds 11th August 1973

"People feel evil things, but nobody ever sings about what's frightening and evil. I mean the world is a right fucking shambles. Anyway, everybody has sung about all the good things. We try to relieve all the tension in the people who listen to us. To get everything out of their bodies – all the evil and everything."

Geezer Butler, Circular, September 1972

SABBATH BACK ON THE ROAD

BLACK SABBATH will make their first British concert tour for over a year this March.

The band will play seven dates opening on March 9 at Glasgow Green's Playhouse.

A second British tour — for three weeks in September — is currently being negotiated.

Dates for the March tour are: Glasgow Green's, March 9; Liverpool Stadium 10; Manchester Hardrock 11; Birmingham Mayfair Ballroom13; Cardiff Sophia Gardens 14; Rainbow 16; Newcastle City Hall 18.

The band's next album will be live cuts taped from their forthcoming European tour. The tour, which starts in mid-February in Amsterdam, takes in Italy, Germany and France. Sabbath will use the Rolling Stones' mobile for the recordings — to be released as their fifth album in mid-April.

The California Jam, 6th April 1974. One of the biggest one-day concerts ever. The line-up included The Eagles, Earth Wind & Fire, Deep Purple and Emerson Lake & Palmer. The attendance has been put at somewhere between 250,000 and 400,000.
Sabbath's set was filmed by ABC TV.

"What people don't realise is that we're not like machines. You've all got your own personal problems as well and on the last tour they were pretty bad."

Tony Iommi, Sounds, 6th January 1973

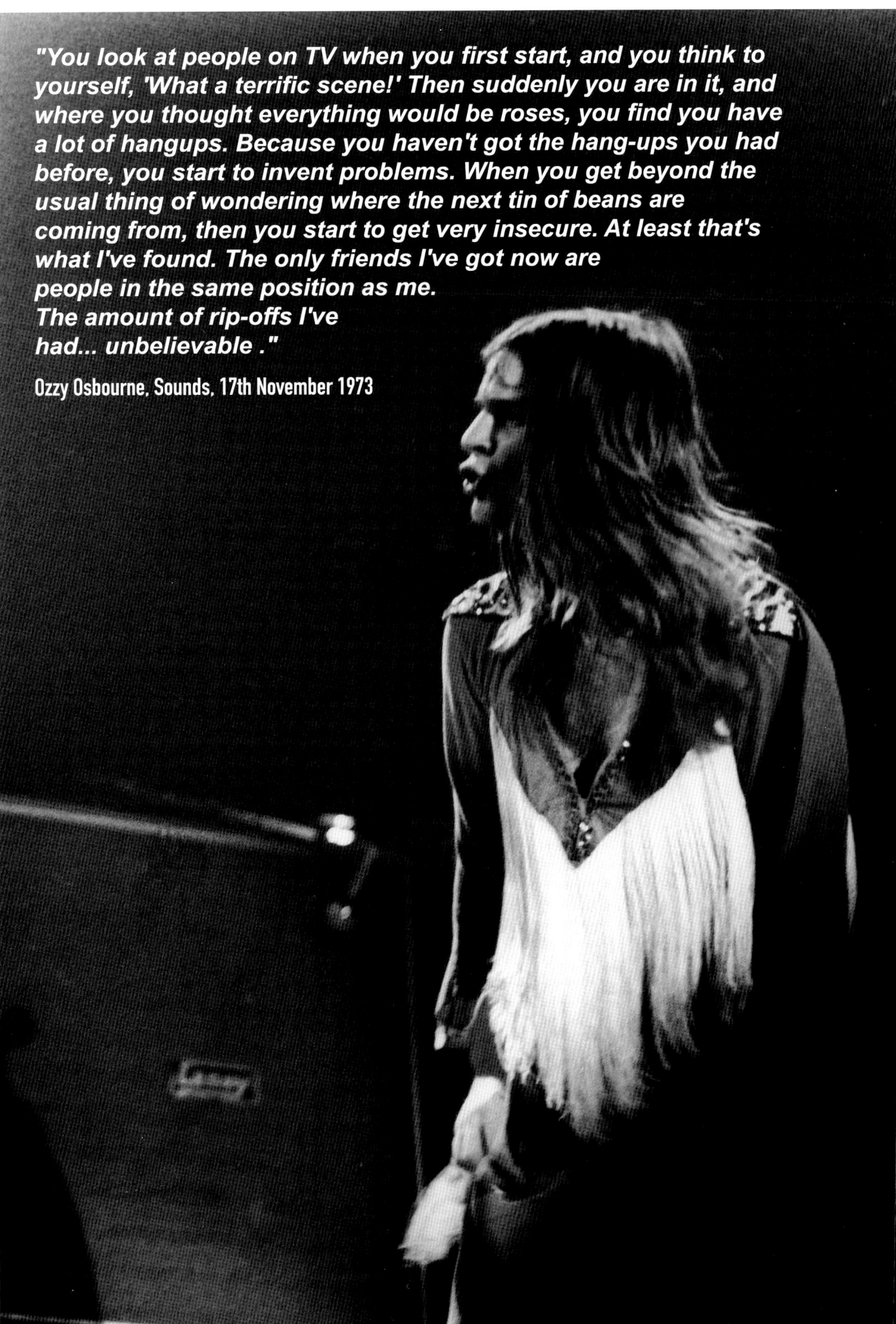

"You look at people on TV when you first start, and you think to yourself, 'What a terrific scene!' Then suddenly you are in it, and where you thought everything would be roses, you find you have a lot of hangups. Because you haven't got the hang-ups you had before, you start to invent problems. When you get beyond the usual thing of wondering where the next tin of beans are coming from, then you start to get very insecure. At least that's what I've found. The only friends I've got now are people in the same position as me. The amount of rip-offs I've had... unbelievable."

Ozzy Osbourne, Sounds, 17th November 1973

"It's nice to tour when you're in the mood for it, and now we're in a position where we can tour when we want to tour; I think you enjoy it a lot more that way. You see we've settled down a lot more with houses and things and it's nice to have some time to ourselves."

Geezer Butler, Sounds 24th March 1973

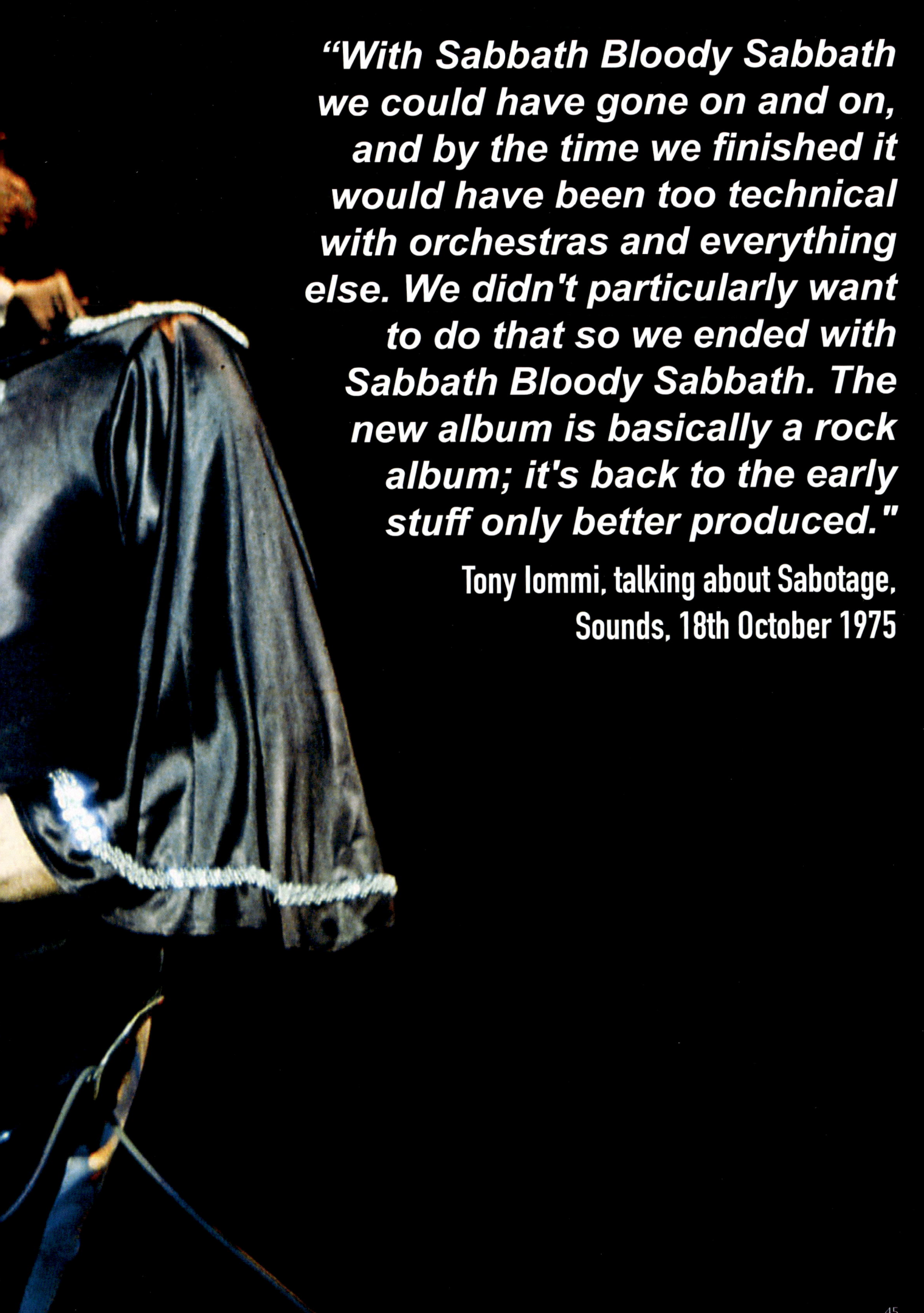

"With Sabbath Bloody Sabbath we could have gone on and on, and by the time we finished it would have been too technical with orchestras and everything else. We didn't particularly want to do that so we ended with Sabbath Bloody Sabbath. The new album is basically a rock album; it's back to the early stuff only better produced."

Tony Iommi, talking about Sabotage, Sounds, 18th October 1975

"After "Masters Of Reality" we really started raking in the coin. It affected us all, being successful and having a lot of money. Looking back what we were playing then wasn't anywhere near our best because we all got into spending a lot of money and the music started to get neglected... The things we got from doing that album have been developed on this new one. We have an orchestra working on it again. Tony's playing a lot more piano and Ozzy's got mellotron which he drives everybody mad with. We've picked up a lot of ideas from "Volume 4". We're also experimenting with things like new guitar and bass sounds which is interesting."

Geezer Butler, Sounds 11th August 1973

Black Sabbath dates

BLACK SABBATH, at present touring America, have now finalised the dates for their British tour in March. They will open at Glasgow Apollo on March 2 and continue at Newcastle City Hall 4, Stafford New Bingley Hall 6, Liverpool Empire 7, Cardiff Capitol Theatre 9, Southampton Gaumont 10, London Hammersmith Odeon 12-13.

The tickets range in price from £1.50 to £2.80 and are on sale at the venues now.

Black Sabbath's new album, Technical Ecstasy, was released by Phonogram last month.

59

61

Ozzy at home in Butt Lane, Ranton, Staffordshire, 1978.

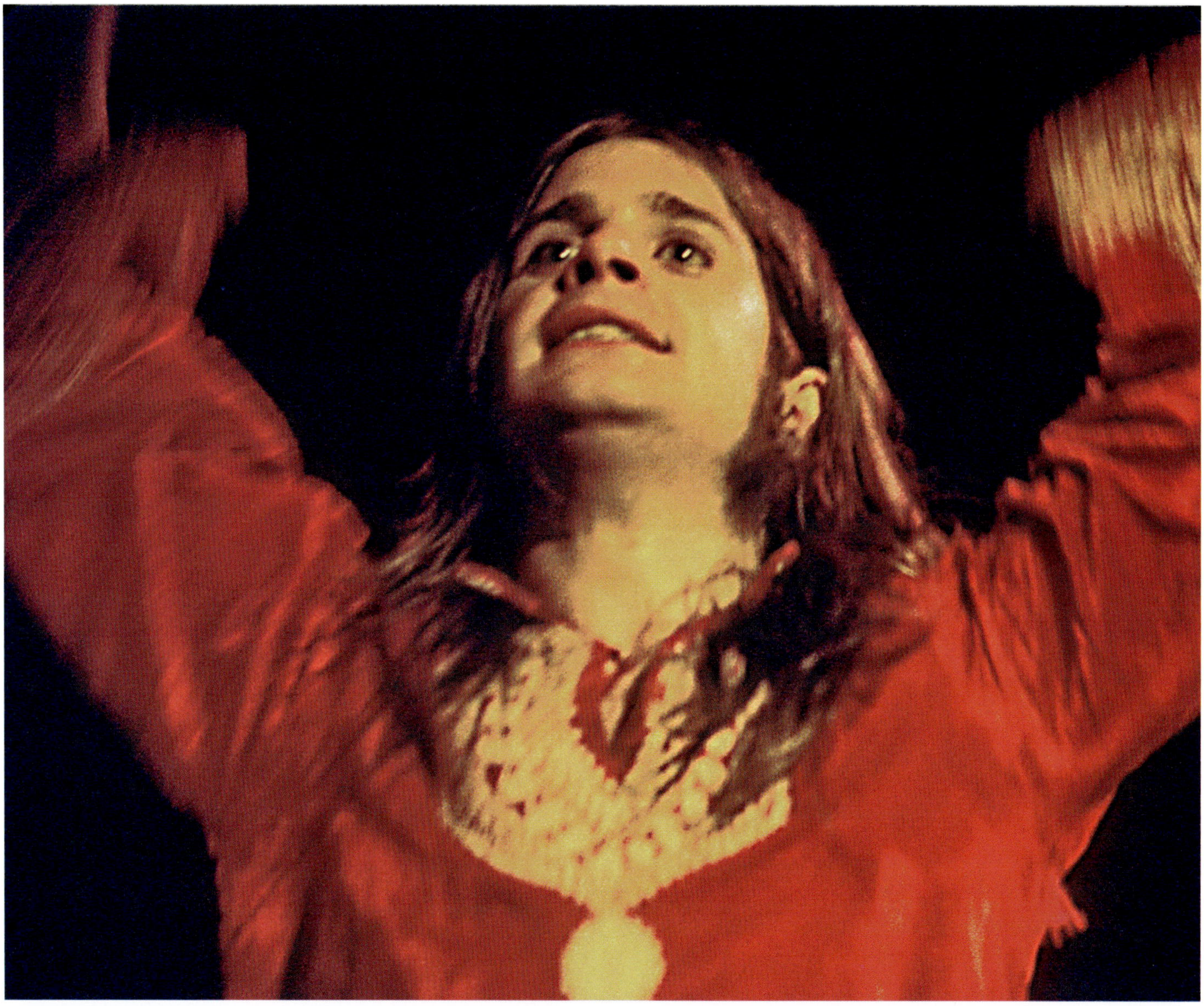

SEPT-3
SHOW 11-15
RACING 19

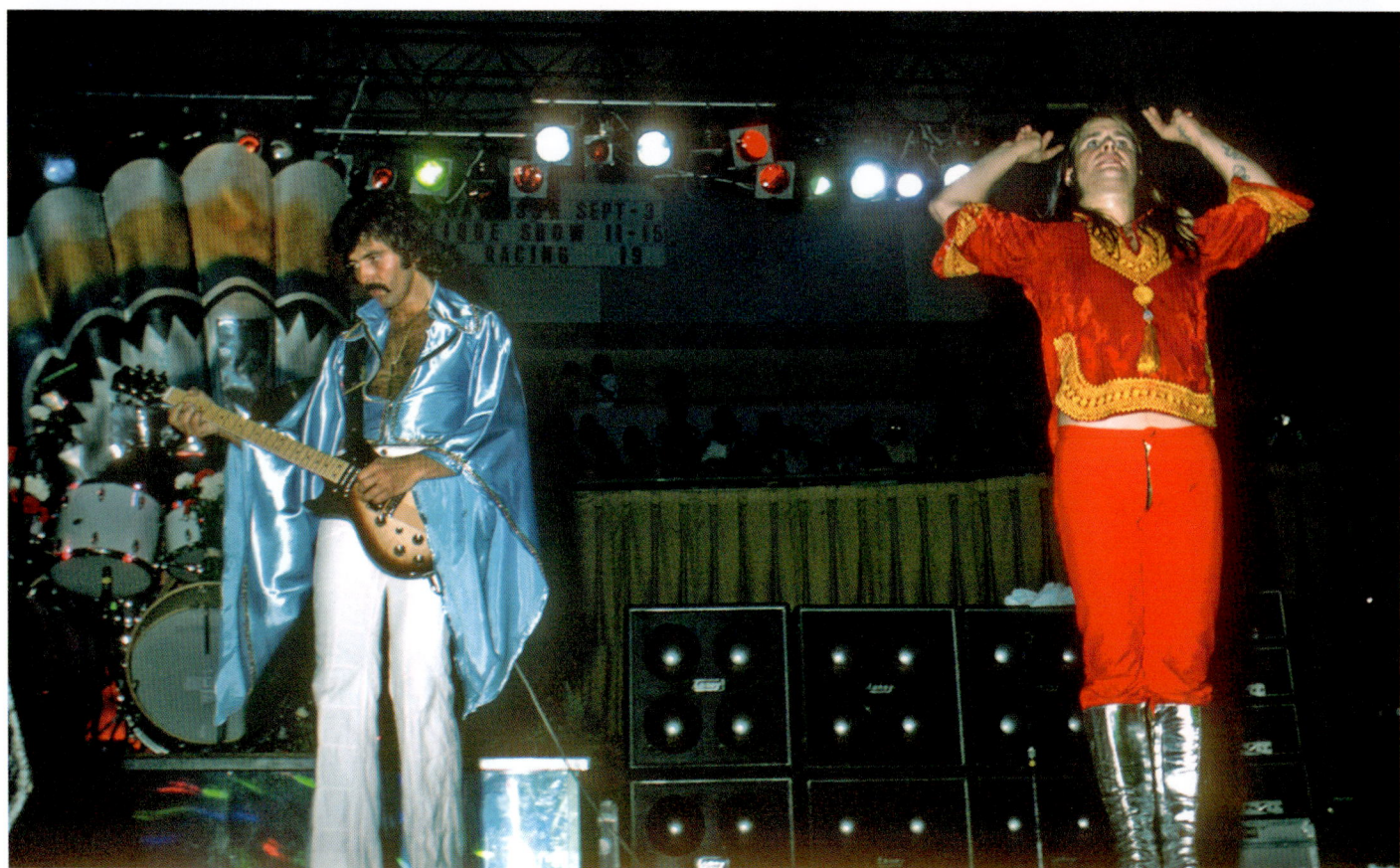

Relaxing at the rehearsal location at Wye Valley, 10th August 1977

At Wye Valley with the silver discs they received for *Technical Ecstasy*.

Ozzy leaves Black Sabbath

OZZY OSBOURNE has quit Black Sabbath and is to start his own band.

The news came this week of the split, which is apparently entirely amicable on both sides and which has often been hinted at in past rumours, but always denied by the group. Osbourne wanted to explore some ideas of his own and is presently forming his own band.

Meanwhile, Sabbath will continue and have already finalised Ozzie's replacement and his name will be announced within the next two weeks. He is believed to be from the Birmingham area, from where the group originated.

Ozzie commented this week: "I am leaving. And there will be a full statement next week. We have got to talk about things yet, until then that is all I can say."

The band was formed in the late Sixties in Birmingham and changed their name from Earth to Black Sabbath for their first album for Vertigo in 1970. Since then they have made six albums, the latest being 'Technical Ecstasy', and had a hit single with 'Paranoid' in 1970.

Sabbath are to record a new album in Canada shortly and it will be released to tie in with their next UK dates next spring.

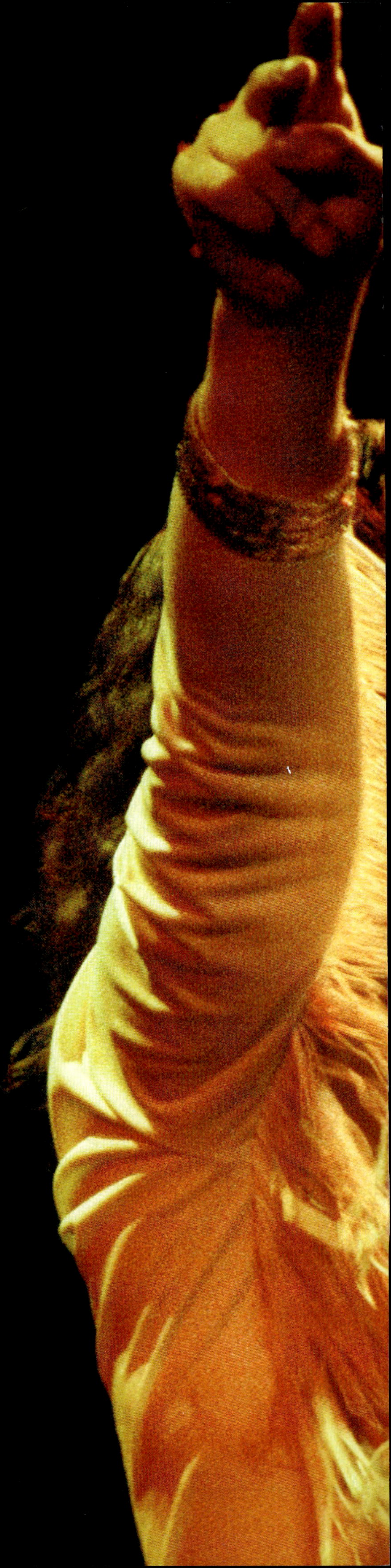

79

"One review of our first album must have been the worst rating ever, and we thought, 'Oh, Christ. This is it.' We were worried if everyone else would think the same."

Tony Iommi, Circular, September 1972

"We'd come offstage and I'd just go straight to the bar. I'd just drink to get out of the way. And that's when you've got to say to yourself, 'Hey man, there's something wrong'. I would have been dead in two or three years if I'd carried on. I know I would. And I don't think anything's worth giving your life up for. I realise I've let a lot of people down because it's never going to be the same again for the people who liked Sabbath then. We haven't left on bad terms. But who knows—it may turn out that way, because time has a weird way of eroding a friendship. I wouldn't say the band screwed me up. But there were a lot of personality clashes."

Ozzy Osbourne, New Musical Express, 3rd December 1977

"When we started doing gigs we were doing things for nothing. We used to travel weeks in a van across Switzerland to do a gig in a brothel or somewhere. But nowadays if somebody writes a song and plays guitar they want to be top of the charts before they've done anything."

Ozzy Osbourne, Sounds, 24th May 1975

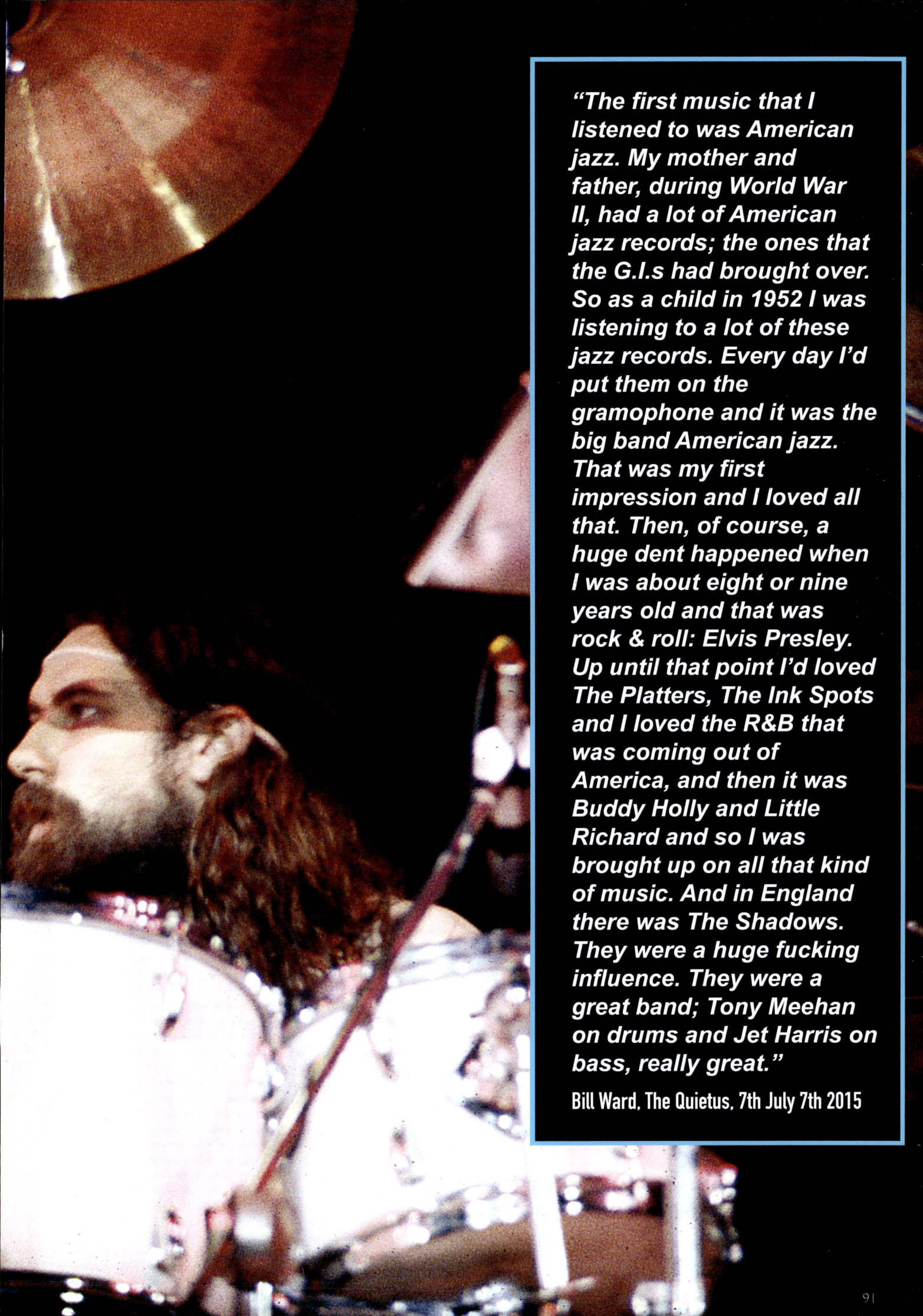

"The first music that I listened to was American jazz. My mother and father, during World War II, had a lot of American jazz records; the ones that the G.I.s had brought over. So as a child in 1952 I was listening to a lot of these jazz records. Every day I'd put them on the gramophone and it was the big band American jazz. That was my first impression and I loved all that. Then, of course, a huge dent happened when I was about eight or nine years old and that was rock & roll: Elvis Presley. Up until that point I'd loved The Platters, The Ink Spots and I loved the R&B that was coming out of America, and then it was Buddy Holly and Little Richard and so I was brought up on all that kind of music. And in England there was The Shadows. They were a huge fucking influence. They were a great band; Tony Meehan on drums and Jet Harris on bass, really great."

Bill Ward, The Quietus, 7th July 7th 2015

"Right before we were supposed to record Never Say Die, Ozzy quit the band. We never wanted him to leave, and I think he wanted to come back—but no one would tell the other how they felt. So we had to bring in another singer and write all new material. Then, two days before we were finally ready to record again, Ozzy decided to come back. But he wouldn't sing any of the stuff we had written without him! Bill had to sing on one track because Ozzy refused to sing it. We ended up having to write in the day so we could record in the evening, and we never had time to review the tracks and make changes. As a result, the album sounds very confused."

Tony Iommi, Guitar World, February 2016

"I overdosed on acid. We were doing a gig in a park in Leamington Spa in 1970. As we were driving into the park, I thought the flowers were trying to get into the car to strangle me. It ended up with me playing on stage thinking I was on a boat and the buildings were waves and I thought my hand was a big spider running up and down my guitar. Acid was a marvellous drug."

Geezer Butler, Classic Rock, 2016

Geezer playing a Rickenbacker that Deep Purple's Glenn Hughes had given him.

"We'd never recorded in a recording studio before. We pulled up, took our gear in, played. Twelve hours it was done. Lo and behold, February comes around, the record comes out, and it's like a major hit. From that moment on my life forever changed. And so I'm really proud of the way it happened because it was no hype. Black Sabbath wasn't like the Bon Jovis of the time. We were just a bunch of guys that were against the grain of society. And we sung about things that people thought back then. But now everyone knows the drugs and war and all that shit, you know?"

Ozzy Osbourne talking about the early days, Esquire, 22nd October 2014

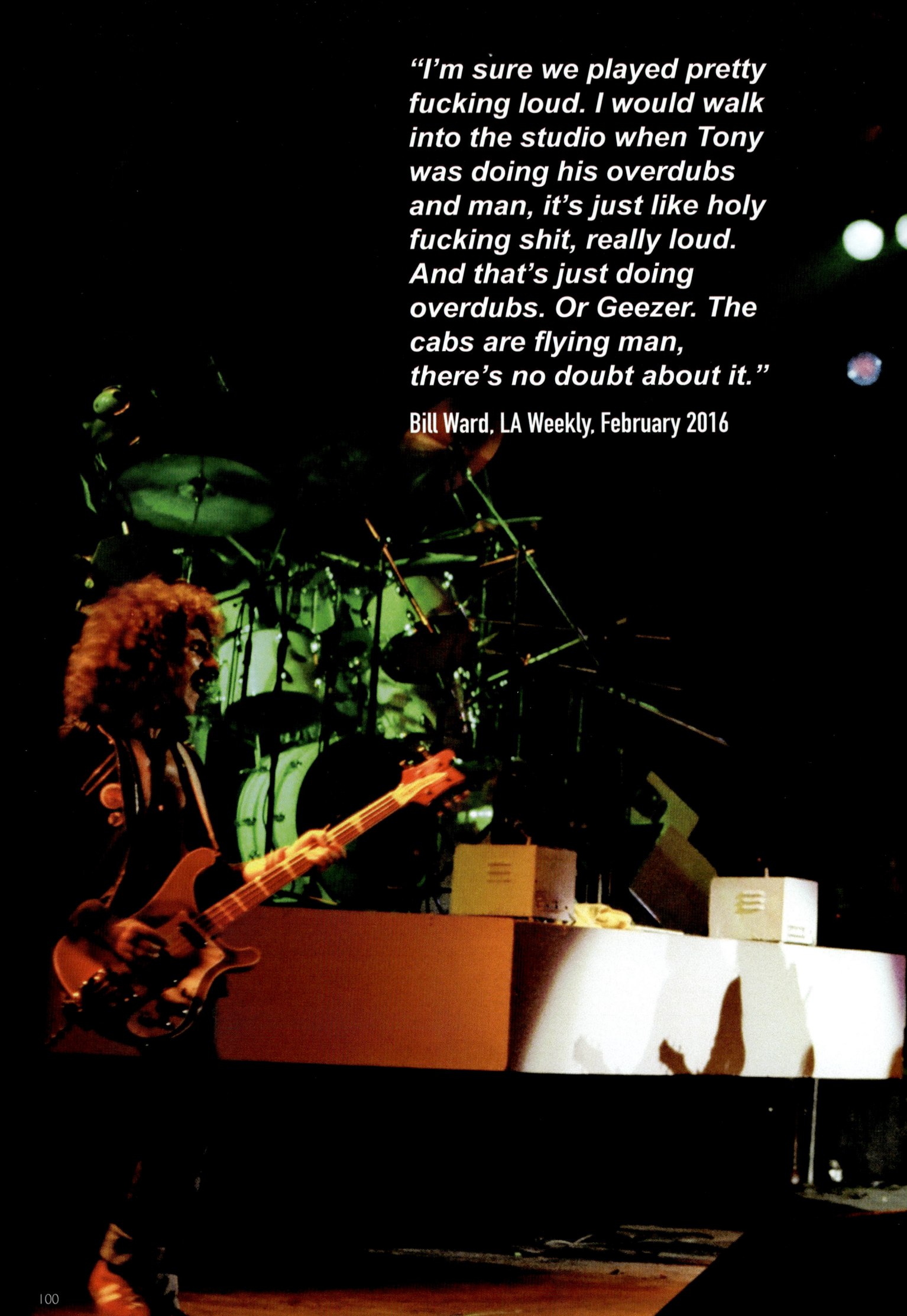

"I'm sure we played pretty fucking loud. I would walk into the studio when Tony was doing his overdubs and man, it's just like holy fucking shit, really loud. And that's just doing overdubs. Or Geezer. The cabs are flying man, there's no doubt about it."

Bill Ward, LA Weekly, February 2016

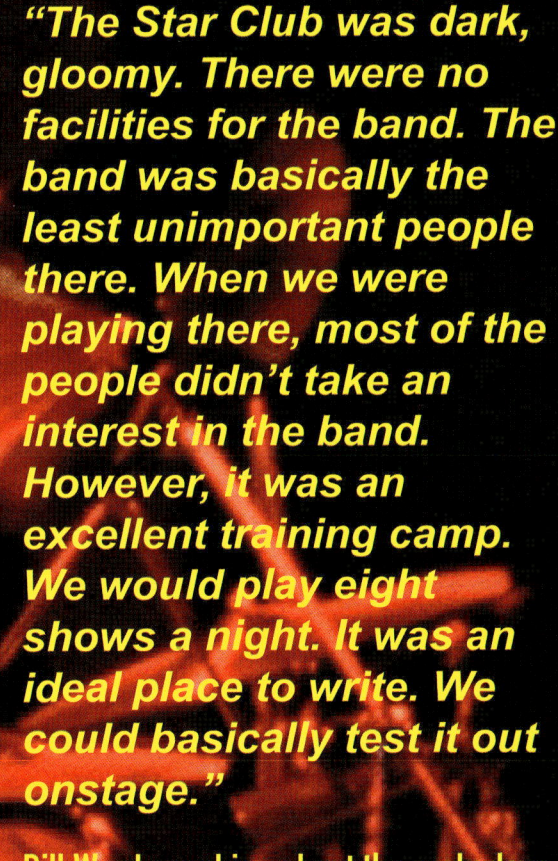

"The Star Club was dark, gloomy. There were no facilities for the band. The band was basically the least unimportant people there. When we were playing there, most of the people didn't take an interest in the band. However, it was an excellent training camp. We would play eight shows a night. It was an ideal place to write. We could basically test it out onstage."

Bill Ward speaking about the early days in 1991

"Geezer would come up with a melodic part and he was the ideal bass player for us. I think we brought out the best in each other. Because none of us were brilliant musicians but as a band it worked. We weren't technically great but we played and we enjoyed what we did. We created a sound, and we created basic riffs that people liked. Well, we liked them anyway!"

Tony Iommi, Music Radar,
21st December 2017

"Money was really scarce in those days, so the whole album was recorded in eight hours on an eight-track machine at Regent Sound in London. We were so pleased to have been given the chance to make a record that the whole experience seemed very luxurious. A record deal in those days was a very big thing."

Tony Iommi about making the first album, Guitar World, February 2016

BLACK SABBATH: 'Hard Road' (Phonogram). Norman Greenbaum's 'Spirit In The Sky' revisited. Not bad though, there's a few spaces between the guitar licks here and there. The Ramones love this band. It's a long hard road to the top, and these guys just got hit by a steamroller.

The Big Sleep

THE RIGOURS of life on-the-road proved rather too much for Sabbath's *Ozzy Osbourne* during the band's current American tour. Obviously suffering from an acute case of the-day-after-the-night-before, he arrived at the latest in a long line of indistinguishable hotel lobbies and decided to grab forty winks before that evening's gig. Apparently, poor old Ozzy had been staying in a room on the fifteenth floor of the hotel the previous night so in his state of non compos mentis he punched the elevator's fifteenth floor button and, when he saw a maid walking out of a convenient room, he just walked in, lay down on the bed and went to sleep.

At show time, Sabbath manager *Albert Chapman* called Ozzy's registered room only to find no sign of him, so he told the waiting fans that Ozzy was sick, and the local police chief that he was missing.

TV Sabbath

BLACK SABBATH make their TV debut with new singer Dave Walker next month — but you'll be able to see it if you live in the Midlands.

They appear on BBC Midlands' ...! on January 6 and ...o songs from their ...lbum, which they ...oronto to record ...

...neduled for April ...band will be

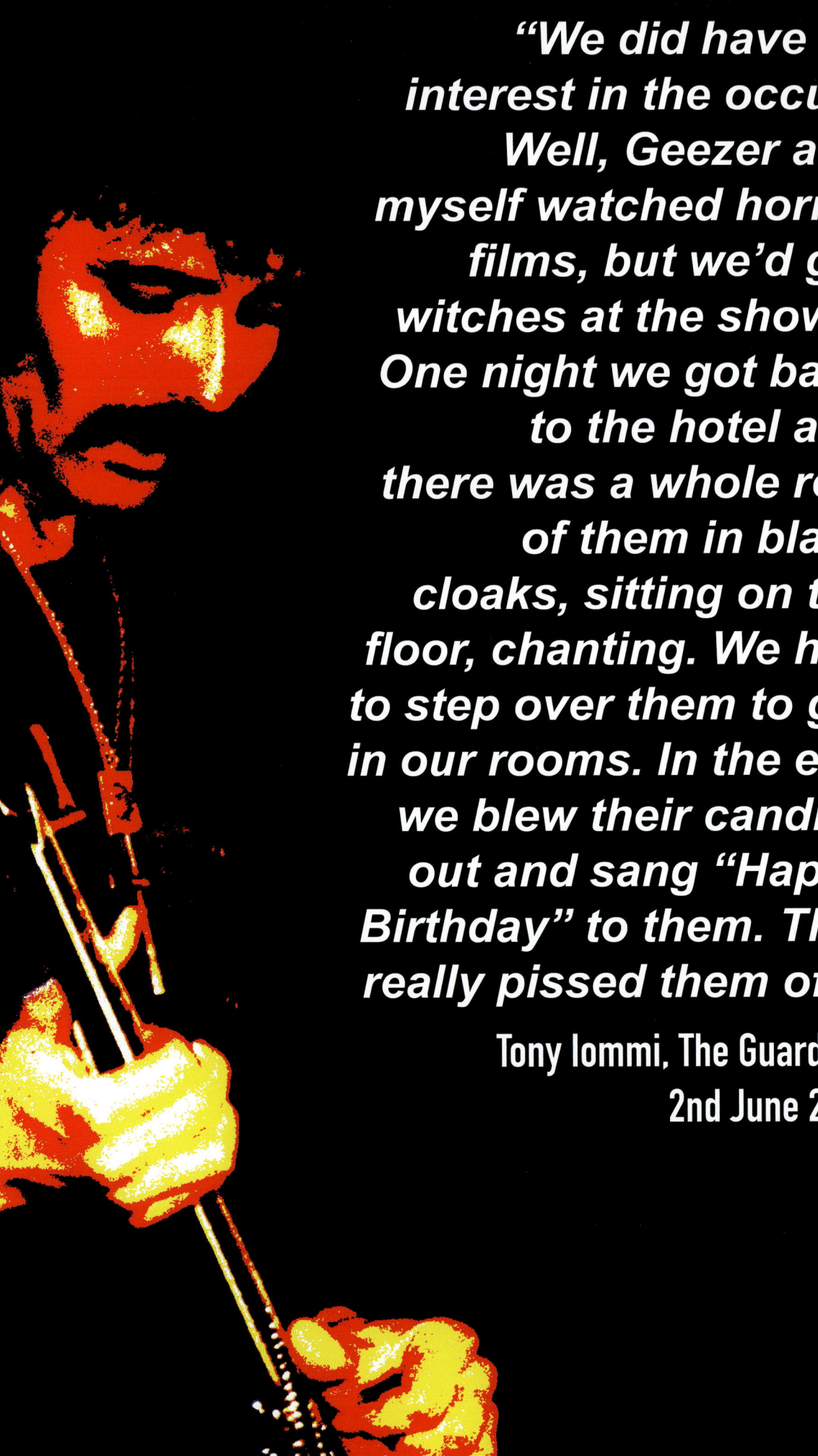

"We did have an interest in the occult. Well, Geezer and myself watched horror films, but we'd get witches at the shows. One night we got back to the hotel and there was a whole row of them in black cloaks, sitting on the floor, chanting. We had to step over them to get in our rooms. In the end we blew their candles out and sang "Happy Birthday" to them. That really pissed them off."

Tony Iommi, The Guardian, 2nd June 2016

Page 6 SOUNDS September 23, 1978

Sabs album

BLACK SABBATH release their new album, 'Never Say Die', next weekend on Phonogram. It naturally includes their hit single of the title track and their next single, 'Hard Road', which is being released at the same time. The first 25,000 copies of the single will be issued in purple vinyl.

The band are currently in the middle of an extensive American tour and return in October for a European tour, for which there are no British dates planned. They then return to the States for more gigs until Christmas.

In the new year there are already plans for the band to tour Japan and Australia so it's unlikely that they'll be touring here again before next spring at the earliest.

"we would just hang out with some of the heads in the Valley and get high, and we went to Laguna to get high as well. Back then, for me there was nothing like dropping some LSD and just letting the surf roll in, you know? Just listening to everybody on the beach. It's a credit to Tony he was able to write this incredible melody and these incredible guitar parts which actually completely summarised 'Laguna Sunrise'. It just couldn't have fit it any better, man."

Bill Ward talking about the period when Vol 4 was recorded. LA Weekly, February 2016

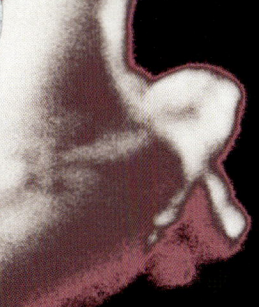

Photo Credits

Front cover: Liverpool Empire 17th June 1978 © Alan Perry.
P2: Mapeldurham Mill, Oxfordshire © Hugh Gilmour.
P5: Hammersmith Odeon, 19th June 1978 © Alan Perry.
P6-9: Piccadilly Circus, London, circa 1970 © Globe Photos/Zumapress.com.
P10-14, 16,17: Concertgebauw, Amsterdam, 4th December 1971 © Laurens Van Houten / Frank White Photo Agency.
P18: Unknown location, © Pictorial Press Ltd / Alamy Stock Photo.
P20-21: 1973, © Pictorial Press Ltd / Alamy Stock Photo.
P22-23: Rai Arena, Amsterdam, 17th April 1977 © Laurens Van Houten / Frank White Photo Agency.
P25-27: Orange Show Auditorium, San Bernardino, 15th September 1975 © Kevin Estrada / Media Punch.
P28-29: Circa 1973 © UtCon Collection / Alamy Stock Photo.
P30-31: (main photo) Hammersmith Odeon, 19th June 1978 © Alan Perry. (Inset) unknown location, © Pictorial Press Ltd / Alamy Stock Photo.
P32-35: California Jam, 6th April 1974 © Pictorial Press Ltd / Alamy Stock Photo.
P36-37: Concertgebauw, Amsterdam, 14th January 1974 © Laurens Van Houten / Frank White Photo Agency.
P38: Hammersmith Odeon, 2nd October 1975 © Steve Emberton.
P39: Concertgebauw, Amsterdam, 14th January 1974 © Laurens Van Houten / Frank White Photo Agency.
P40, 41: Hammersmith Odeon, 2nd October 1975 © Steve Emberton.
P42-47: Rai Arena, Amsterdam, 17th April 1977 © Laurens Van Houten / Frank White Photo Agency.
P48, 49: Hammersmith Odeon, 2nd October 1975 © Steve Emberton.
P50: Amsterdam 1975 © Laurens Van Houten / Frank White Photo Agency.
P51, 52: Hammersmith Odeon, 2nd October 1975 © Steve Emberton.
P53: Amsterdam 1975 © Laurens Van Houten / Frank White Photo Agency.
P54: Concertgebauw, Amsterdam, 4th December 1971 © Laurens Van Houten / Frank White Photo Agency.
P56-7: Concertgebauw, Amsterdam, 14th January 1974 © Laurens Van Houten / Frank White Photo Agency.
P58-63: Assembly Center, Tulsa, 22nd October 1976 © Richard Galbraith.
P64: (main) Hammersmith Odeon, 2nd October 1975 © Steve Emberton. (Inset) © Granamour Weems Collection / Alamy Stock Photo.
P65: Ranton, Staffordshire 1978 © Birmingham Mail / Reach Publishing Services Limited.
P66: Circa 1974 © Pictorial Press Ltd / Alamy Stock Photo.
P67-73: Wye Valley, 10th August 1977 © Birmingham Mail / Reach Publishing Services Limited.
P74-107: Liverpool Empire 17th June 1978 / Hammersmith Odeon, 19th June 1978 © Alan Perry. (Inset, top right, P103: Assembly Center, Tulsa, 18th September 1978 © Richard Galbraith.
P108-111: Assembly Center, Tulsa, 18th September 1978 © Richard Galbraith.
P112-113: Hammersmith Odeon, 19th June 1978 © Alan Perry.
P114: Liverpool Empire 17th June 1978 © Alan Perry.
P116, 117: Hammersmith Odeon, 19th June 1978 © Alan Perry.
P118: Circa 1975 © Pictorial Press Ltd / Alamy Stock Photo.
P119: © Pictorial Press Ltd / Alamy Stock Photo.
P120-121: Hammersmith Odeon, 19th June 1978 © Alan Perry.
P122: Circa 1975 © Pictorial Press Ltd / Alamy Stock Photo.
P123: Liverpool Empire 17th June 1978 © Alan Perry.
P124: Assembly Center, Tulsa, 18th September 1978 © Richard Galbraith.
P125-126: Hammersmith Odeon, 19th June 1978 © Alan Perry.
Back Cover: Assembly Center, Tulsa, 22nd October 1976 © Richard Galbraith

"When Ozzy left in 1979. Bill and me literally cried to each other. Ozzy was a person we'd grown up with. It was something that had to happen, but it was the end of an era."
Geezer Classic Rock, 2016